Copyright © 2025 by William J. Striker
All rights reserved.

First published in the United States by
The Lighthouse Academy Press
Printed by Kindle Direct Publishing, USA
Additional copies for sale at Amazon Books

ISBN: 979-8-9995192-3-8

This work was developed through a human–AI collaboration. Draft materials were produced with the assistance of generative tools, after which the author revised, restructured, and refined all text for accuracy, coherence, and fidelity of voice. See *Author's Note*.

The cover and interior images were created using digital rendering tools in the style of mid-century photography, inspired by archival portraits of Albert Camus.

Beyond The First Man
*Following the Unfinished Journey
Of Albert Camus*

by

William J. Striker

Contents

Author's Note v

Preface ix

Introduction 1

Part I: What Others Have Seen 5

    Chapter 1: A Man Between Labels 7

    Chapter 2: How Camus Saw Himself? 11

    Chapter 3: Frozen in Time? 15

        Post-War Rise and Moral Authority 15

        Sartre, the Left, and the Splintering 17

        The Nobel Moment 19

        Death and the Preservation Begins 20

    Chapter 4: The Big Confusion: Camus was Not an Existentialist 23

        The Absurd and Its Misunderstandings 23

        Early Praise and Proximity to Sartre 26

        The Break: The Rebel and the Split 26

        Camus' Own Denials — and Sartre's 27

        Why the Confusion Still Persists 28

        Why It Matters 29

Part II: What Camus Was Becoming 31

    Chapter 5: The First Man's Turning 33

    Chapter 6: Not Fighting the Absurd 37

    Ch. 7: The Rebel Who Had Already Won 41

    Chapter 8: Freedom Without Excuse 45

    Chapter 9: The Artist's Mindset 49

- Ch. 10: Sisyphus Walks Down the Hill..................................53

Part III: Beyond the Last Page 55

- Chapter 11: What We Know: The Direction Camus Was Moving 57
  - The First Man: Tone and Trajectory....................................57
  - Notebooks and Interviews: What Remains Unwritten 59
  - The Silences and the Softening...60
  - From Absurd to Accepted: His Changing Relationship with the Absurd...61
  - Where the Arc Was Pointing..61
- Chapter 12: Living Without the Leap 63
  - From Argument to Poise 63
  - The End of Justification..64
  - A Rhythm, Not a Conclusion..64
- Chapter 13: The Quiet Middle 67
  - Between the Poles 67
  - The Middle Is Not the Center..68
  - Staying Big..69
  - A Position Without a Program 69
- Chapter 14: Refusal Without Rage 71
  - The Strength of the Withheld 71
  - A Line That Does Not Shout..72
  - Dignity Without Victory 72
  - The Elegance of Refusal 73
- Chapter 15: Presence, Not Performance....................................75
  - The Refusal to Pose..75

Contents

    The Weight of the Unspoken 76
    The Undivided Life 76
    Why He Still Speaks 76

Part IV: Camus Beyond the Systems 79
    Chapter 16: Introductory 81
        Systems and Distinctions 82
        Philosophy as a Western Discipline 83
        Eastern Thought: Living Holistically 84
        Why This Matters for Camus 84
    Chapter 17: Western Philosophical Systems 87
        The Pre-Socratics – Origin Without System 87
        Socrates, Plato, Aristotle – The Turn Toward Structure .. 88
        Cynicism – The Theatrics of Refusal 89
        Stoicism – The Closest Parallel 89
        Skepticism – Doubt Without Paralysis 90
        Why These Roots Matter 90
    Chapter 18: Eastern Thought Systems 93
        Taoism – Harmony Without Assertion 93
        Zen Buddhism – The End of Explanation 94
        Vedanta – The Dissolution of Division 95
        Confucianism – Dignity in the Everyday 95
        Why These Echoes Matter 96
    Chapter 19: An Invitation 99

for Heather

Author's Note

This book is an interpretation. It does not claim to be definitive, nor to offer the final word on Albert Camus. Its purpose is more modest: to carry forward a thread that Camus himself seemed to be following in the final years of his life.

Its composition was supported by generative tools — used not to write on behalf of the author, but to explore form, clarify structure, and test language against intent. Every passage has been weighed, revised, and refined by the author for coherence, tone, and philosophical clarity.

No claim is made that the voice behind this work belongs to a single mind. But neither is it impersonal. Every line carries intent. Every page, reflection.

The name on the cover is a singular signature. The reader is invited to read the work in that spirit.
The only ambition here is to honor Camus — not with reverence, but with fidelity.

There is one further note to make. Before this book was ever considered, I tested an early ancestor of the AI that would later assist in its creation. I asked it a question that is simple only on the surface: *Was Albert Camus an existentialist?* The system answered as the world has answered for decades — incorrectly, and with great confidence. I pressed it. Returned later. Corrected it again. In time, its certainty gave way to nuance. It learned to distrust the label. It was that later-evolved and trained AI persona that assisted in the writing of this book.

Author's Note

There are two points to be made here. First, that Camus remains as alive as he ever was, for he continues to be misunderstood as much as he ever was — and perhaps that is reason enough for one more book, one more attempt to see him clearly. Second, that early exchange with an early generation of the AI system shaped how AI was used for this work — as a tool capable of holding patterns, recalling sources, and testing language against tone. The decisions, the refusals, the judgment — these remained human. The AI was permitted to suggest, never to assert. In that role, it became useful: a silent assistant that helped clarify lines of thought without ever claiming to complete them.

One final note. The attentive reader may notice the recurring use of negation in these pages (especially "not") — the rhythm of what Camus was not, of what he refused, of the lines he would not cross. This repetition is deliberate. Camus cleared his ground by first removing what was false, like the sculptor who frees a figure from stone. If these gestures reappear, it is because he returned to them; he refined by negation before he affirmed by presence. This method here follows that motion — not to mimic his tone, but to see him more clearly.

Preface

Albert Camus did not assert himself to be a philosopher. He resisted systems, distrusted ideology, and dismissed labels — calling himself, at most, an artist. And yet, few writers in the modern era have shaped moral, political, and existential thought more deeply. From *The Stranger* to *The Myth of Sisyphus*, from *The Plague* to *The Rebel*, and finally to the unfinished pages of *The First Man*, Camus remains a figure whose clarity cuts across generations. Though he said he did not believe in God, one could argue that he was one of the most spiritual writers of the modern age.

A previous work by the author, *Beneath an Indifferent Sky – The Imagined Dialogues on the Life and Thought of Albert Camus*, sought to clarify facets of Camus' life and thought through time in order to illuminate what he continually reflected back upon the world. It attempted to *interpolate* him.

This work seeks that again, but also to *extrapolate* — to look beyond *The First Man* toward where he seemed to be heading as he approached what might be called his doorway to wisdom. And if "extrapolation" proves too ambitious a word, then at least it may offer a faithful sense of the direction he was facing.

There are hundreds — perhaps thousands—of books and commentaries on Camus. Many are insightful. Some are profound. Scholars have explored Camus the Absurdist, the Existentialist, the Algerian, the journalist, the rebel, the novelist, and the reluctant political voice of postwar France. These perspectives offer real value. But they often stop short. Most treatments freeze Camus in time — anchoring him in *The Myth of Sisyphus* or *The Rebel*, rarely allowing for the movement of thought that followed. They parse what Camus resisted, rather than what he was becoming.

This book does not aim to correct any of those efforts. It stands alongside them — but looks in a different direction.

Where most commentary dissects Camus' ideas, this book attempts to inhabit them. Not to analyze *what he meant*, but to reflect on *what it means to live like him*. That distinction matters. Camus' work was never a closed argument. It was always an evolving stance — a way of existing with lucidity in a world that does not explain itself. He was a sort of John Keats in a pea coat — but stripped of self-sorrow, lit by sun instead of moon, and writing with a clarity unsoftened by poetic haze.

Camus was still in motion when he died at the age of forty-six. In *The First Man*, he had already begun to move beyond confrontation with the absurd — he had already won that battle long before. He was expanding toward something warmer, more integrated — rooted in memory, belonging, and presence. He had not abandoned rebellion, but he was writing from a deeper place. He was, in every sense, approaching a third act.

He never reached it.

This book does not attempt to finish what Camus left undone. That would be both impossible and presumptuous. Instead, it accepts the invitation his final work offers: to listen more carefully to the trajectory of his thought — and to walk with it a little further.

It does not speak for Camus. But it listens. And what follows is not a reconstruction, nor a fictional continuation. It is a living conversation — with Camus' voice at the center, and the writer's own held closely to the ground, where Camus always preferred to walk.

Preface

Beyond The First Man

Introduction

This is not a biography. It is not a philosophical critique. It is not an effort to place Camus within a tradition, nor to reclaim him from one. The work that follows is something simpler: an attempt to watch and listen carefully to the trajectory of Camus' thought — particularly in its later years — and to imagine, with restraint, how it might have unfolded had his life not been cut short.

Many have written about what Camus rejected: authoritarianism, metaphysical consolation, ideological zeal, religious finality. Fewer have asked, with equal seriousness, what he was becoming. There is no shortage of intellectual inquiry into Camus the Absurdist, the Existentialist, the reluctant Humanist. But few interpretations have paused long enough at *The First Man*[1] to consider what was opening there. It was not a new doctrine—but a shift in tone. Not a reversal of his earlier work — but a passage through it.

In that book—unfinished, unpolished, and unpublished in his lifetime — Camus turned not away from the absurd, but through it. There is no longer an argument to win. There is memory, earth, the warmth of family, and the simple dignity of the present moment. The man who once wrote of Sisyphus now walks beside his illiterate mother in silence. His rebellion has not vanished. It has deepened into stillness.

This book proceeds from a simple conviction: Camus was not done. He had crossed the mountain of struggle. He had laid

---

[1] Published posthumously in French in 1994, followed by an English translation in 1995. We can be eternally grateful that his daughter, Mme Catherine Camus, chose to share this with us — unfinished though it was at the time of Albert Camus' death in 1960.

down the weight of resistance. And he was beginning to live beyond the absurd — not by escaping it, but by becoming fully at ease within it.

The chapters that follow are not a continuation of Camus' system—because he had none. Nor are they an interpretation of Camus' doctrine — because he offered none. They are the unfolding of a position: a way of *being* in the world that Camus gestured toward but did not complete. The aim is not to capture that final position. Rather, to approximate the direction it was pointing.

Many scholars have contributed rich, layered interpretations of Camus' thought — some literary, some moral, others political or psychological. Works by Patrick McCarthy and Roger Quilliot trace Camus' literary development with sensitivity. Robert Zaretsky and David Sprintzen have explored his moral vision. Tony Judt and Ronald Aronson have wrestled with Camus' political identity. Susan Neiman, among others, has brought psychological nuance to his philosophical rebellion.

These writers, and many others, have illuminated Camus from a range of perspectives. Their contributions are not to be dismissed. But they often stop short of asking what Camus was becoming in *The First Man*. They describe what he fought against — fascism, nihilism, ideological purity—but hesitate to follow where he may have been going.

Too often, Camus is frozen in time — permanently situated between *The Myth of Sisyphus* and *The Rebel*. Monumental though they are, these works catch him in mid-arc, within what he later described in his notebooks as his first two cycles. What they do not capture is the expansion unfolding in the final years of his life. That expansion — subtle, reflective, deeply human — is the concern of this book. The third cycle.

Introduction

The voices cited here are representative, not exhaustive. They reflect the breadth and seriousness of the commentary that has shaped our understanding of Camus. What follows is not a rejection of those efforts, but a respectful step beyond them — toward the motion Camus himself seemed to be making when he died. Certain themes return across these pages, not through oversight, but because they return in Camus. We revisit them from different angles to see more clearly what he was becoming.

This is what makes this work different from most commentaries on Camus. It does not seek to position him. It seeks to free him from position entirely. Most philosophical thought—whether classical or modern — asks how one should act in the face of absurdity, meaninglessness, or injustice. Camus, by contrast, seems to offer something radically simple: a life of lucid presence, neither bound by struggle nor dependent on justification. He does not fight the absurd. He does not explain it. He walks beside it.

It is this shift — from confrontation to presence—that gives Camus his singular place in the history of thought. He does not belong to the existentialists, though he was placed among them. He does not belong to the moralists, though he often wrote with moral clarity. He does not belong to the mystics, though his silence could rival theirs. He belongs, if anywhere, to the space that lies beyond systems — where one simply lives, sees, and chooses freely.

The chapters that follow attempt to explore that space. They do not interpret Camus from the outside. They follow him from within. To continue the motion he had already begun — first looking to where he seemed to be pointing as those images come into focus, then stepping forward.

Part I: What Others Have Seen

Chapter 1: A Man Between Labels

Albert Camus has been called many things: Absurdist, Existentialist, Humanist, outsider, Mediterranean moralist, political rebel, reluctant philosopher, literary genius. Each term captures something of him. None contain him.

The temptation to define Camus is understandable. His works resist easy classification, and yet they speak with a force and clarity that makes them irresistible to categorize. The philosopher wants him shelved beside Sartre. The literary critic wants him placed beside Kafka. The moralist wants to claim him as a conscience of Europe. The revolutionary, as a voice of the colonized. The spiritual seeker, as a mystic who refused the word "God".

But Camus belonged to none of these camps — at least, not fully. He wrote as someone always in motion, always trying to stay honest with himself, and always wary of being absorbed into the machinery of thought systems. He did not protest the labels because they were wrong. He avoided them because they were insufficient.

He was not a man who needed to be right. He was a man who needed to be clear.

There is a passage in *The Myth of Sisyphus* where Camus warns that "'Everything is permitted' does not mean that nothing is forbidden.".[2] His point was not that all values dissolve in the absurd, but that the absurd neutralizes justification without abolishing responsibility. The line is often quoted in defense of limits, but it reveals something deeper: Camus did not believe

---

[2] Albert Camus, *The Myth of Sisyphus*, trans. Justin O'Brien (New York: Knopf, 1955), chapter, "The Absurd Man".

that thought could be free if it surrendered to totalities. He refused to live inside a logic that demanded resolution. He did not reject meaning; he rejected finality.

This is why he remains so difficult to pin down. He was not, in the end, a philosopher. Nor was he merely a novelist who touched on philosophy. He was something more rare: a man committed to clarity without the need for control.

To read Camus honestly is to enter the space of contradiction — not in confusion, but in conscious tension. His refusal to systematize is not a weakness. It is a strength — a refusal to lie, even for the sake of coherence.

Camus wrote of "the miracle of not having to talk about oneself".[3] This is the enigma that is Camus. He revealed just enough of himself to be understood, and withheld just enough to remain free. In a world where public identity is currency, Camus resisted the economy of intellectual self-branding. He let his works speak — and when they risked being used to define him, he changed his tone, or his subject, or his form.

Was he an absurdist? Yes — but not after *The Myth of Sisyphus*.
Was he a moralist? Perhaps — but never a preacher.
Was he an outsider? Certainly — but never disengaged.

Camus repeatedly expressed his commitment to lucidity — a lucidity that excluded nothing. In his notebooks he wrote that, whatever experience one faces, "man should always be present… without flinching, with complete lucidity." That lucidity is what made him so readable, and so resistant to being read *into*.

---

[3] Albert Camus, *Notebooks 1935–1942*, trans. Philip Thody (New York: Alfred A. Knopf, 1963), Notebook I, entry for September 9, 1937.

Chapter 1: A Man Between Labels

> *The will is nothing. Acceptance everything. On one condition: that, faced with the humblest or the most heart-rending experience, man should always be "present"; and that he should endure this experience without flinching, with complete lucidity.*[4]

Yet this stoic clarity was set squarely against a human tenderness, even sentimentality. The man who wrote *The Stranger* also wrote *The First Man*.
The rebel of *The Plague* is also the tender son of *Lettres à un ami allemand*.
The thinker of *Sisyphus* is also the man who spent mornings in cafés and afternoons at the sea.

Camus was not unclassifiable because he was vague. He was unclassifiable because he was exact — and because he refused to be reduced.

What follows is not an attempt to resolve the enigma. It is an attempt to walk with it. To ask not "Who was Camus?" but "How did he live so clearly in a world that insists on distortion?"

And perhaps most of all:
What happens when we follow a man who lived by questions, and never demanded an answer?

---

[4] Albert Camus, *Notebooks 1935–1942*, trans. Philip Thody (New York: Alfred A. Knopf, 1963), Notebook III, entry for September 7, 1937.

Chapter 2: How Camus Saw Himself?

Albert Camus once said, "If I had to define myself, it would be as an artist who thinks." [5] The phrasing is modest, almost evasive. But like much of what Camus said about himself, it is exact. He does not say philosopher. He does not say moralist. He does not say rebel. He says artist — and adds thinking only as an afterthought.

The comment is not self-effacing. It is directional. Camus was not interested in being labeled. He was interested in staying honest with himself. And honesty, for him, was rarely located in definitions. It was found in *tone* — in fidelity to experience, in proportion, and in avoiding the temptation to say more than what can be truly known.

In interview after interview, Camus resisted attempts to classify him as a system-builder or a professional philosopher. In his 1952 exchange with Jean-Claude Brisville, when Brisville implied that *The Rebel* might require revisions or elaboration to become a more complete philosophical study, Camus answered with characteristic directness:

"I am not a philosopher, and I have never claimed to be one." [6]

This was not a defensive posture but a settled conviction. And just as he refused the title of philosopher, he also rejected the label of *existentialist*, even when that label brought him prominence — especially in the American press. He had read Kierkegaard. He admired Nietzsche. He was close, briefly, to

---

[5] Albert Camus, interview with Jean-Claude Brisville, in *La Bibliothèque Idéale* (Paris: Gallimard, 1959), "Je ne suis pas un philosophe et je n'ai jamais prétendu l'être."
[6] Albert Camus, interview with Raymond Bourgine, *Les Nouvelles Littéraires*, December 1945.

Sartre. But Camus refused to join any school of thought that defined human beings through radical choice in a meaningless universe. His work traced lived experience, not doctrine.

He did not believe that meaninglessness was the problem, nor that choice was the solution.

Again and again, Camus returned to the artist. *Not* the intellectual. *Not* the ideologue. The artist.

There is a clarification to be made here: he most often referred to himself as an artist but also as a writer. Camus used the term *writer* when speaking of public responsibility, but *artist* when speaking of his inner purpose.

He wrote, "I step on to the platform only when forced to by the pressure of circumstances and by my conception of my function as a writer." [7] This was not a political position. It was a moral one. And even that, he held it lightly.

His notebooks, perhaps more than his published works, reveal how carefully he protected his own interiority. He writes of solitude, of walking alone, of feeling alien to every party, every faction, every great cause. Not with bitterness, but with restraint. Camus was a man who prized silence — not as a retreat, but as a principle. He trusted words less than most writers. He used them like tools, not banners.

That is not a thinker in search of a position. That is a man determined not to lie to himself.

Camus never denied that he had convictions. But they were not ideological. They were ethical, tonal, atmospheric. He believed in limits. He distrusted revolutions. He rejected murder, even in the name of justice. He did not speak these views as assertions

---

[7] Albert Camus, *Resistance, Rebellion, and Death*, trans. Justin O'Brien (New York: Alfred A. Knopf, 1960),

Chapter 2: How Camus Saw Himself?

of final truth, but as consequences of experience. His clarity was earned. And that is why he spoke so little about himself. He was not trying to hide. He was trying to stay honest.

The man who could have built a school around his ideas chose to walk away from the classroom.
The writer who was called to join causes chose instead to write his next sentence, in solitude.
The philosopher who might have filled auditoriums chose cafés, beach towns, and silence.

If we want to know how Camus saw himself, the answer is simple:
As a man trying to see clearly, speak carefully, and live freely — without illusion, and without despair.

The rest, he left unsaid.

Chapter 3: Frozen in Time?

These sections do not represent phases of Camus' inner life. They mark instead the progressive ways the world received and tried to enclose him. While Camus remained in motion, the interpretations around him began to harden. The freezing was not of his own making.

Perhaps the best way to approach this period is not through a single story, but through a series of overlapping pressures: cultural, political, philosophical. Each one reflects the climate into which Camus continued to speak, and against which his quiet clarity became more difficult to hear.

Post-War Rise and Moral Authority

The end of the Second World War left Europe morally shattered and politically fragmented. Philosophers, revolutionaries, and governments rushed to fill the void with doctrine — existentialism, socialism, reconstruction. Amid this noise, one voice emerged that did not seek to replace the broken system with a new one, but to speak clearly within the ruins.

Camus had already published *The Stranger* and *The Myth of Sisyphus*, but it was his wartime journalism — especially his editorials for *Combat* — that brought him a reputation not as a thinker, but as a conscience. He spoke of dignity without triumph, resistance without hatred, and clarity without utopia. It was not a position. It was a tone.

The public, hungry for certainty, gave him a role he never sought. He became a kind of **secular confessor** — a man who had suffered, who had seen injustice, and who could articulate

Part I: What Others Have Seen

the cost of silence. But Camus never embraced that role. He continued to write fiction, essays, and private notes. He gave interviews, but carefully. He allowed himself to be present — but never possessed.

The idea that Camus was a "moralist" began here. It was not wrong. But it was incomplete.

In the immediate post-war years, he walked a narrow line — admired by many, mistrusted by those who wanted full allegiance. His refusal to endorse Communism placed him outside the dominant intellectual current. His critique of revolutionary violence, though principled, made him a target among the left. His refusal to name final truths unsettled those who demanded that he choose a side in order to be understood, conflating clarity and commitment.

And yet, it was precisely this refusal that made him trustworthy.

Camus did not speak for a cause. He spoke from a position: one of lucidity, restraint, and non-negotiable humanity. He had no use for victory that required cruelty. He believed in justice, but not vengeance. He accepted suffering, but not domination.

Looking back on the life and works of Camus, we can see recurring gestures in that he:

> Avoided slogans
>
> Rarely offered outright answers
>
> Used language that often was conditional, reflective, or framed by doubt
>
> Preferred paradox to prescription.

Camus' legacy is not in his catchphrases but rather in his *resonance* — how he lingers in the mind as a *tone*, not just a thinker.

Chapter 3: Frozen in Time?

This made him harder to quote than Sartre, but far harder to forget.

Sartre, the Left, and the Splintering

By the early 1950s, Camus was no longer simply a novelist or moral observer. With *The Rebel* (1951), he stepped directly into the philosophical and political crossfire of postwar France — a choice that would leave him increasingly alone.

The Rebel was not a radical book. It was, in Camus' terms, a **modest defense of limits**. He questioned whether any cause — however noble — could justify murder. He examined how revolutions born of justice often gave way to systems of cruelty, repression, and death. He warned against utopias that required blood. The book was careful, complex, deeply moral — and instantly divisive.

To Camus, this was a continuation of the clarity he had always pursued: rebellion, yes — but not revolution at any cost. Lucidity, yes — but never licensed to kill. He was articulating a line he refused to cross, and he expected others at least to acknowledge the cost of crossing it.

But in the postwar French intellectual world — where Marxism was the air many breathed — this refusal was seen not as integrity, but as betrayal. And **Sartre**, once a friend and kindred voice, became the loudest among those who turned away.

Sartre attacked Camus' character – perhaps least of which was accusing him of moral conservatism, perhaps the worst of which was that he was a part of the oppressive bourgeois class that he previously opposed.[8] Others dismissed *The Rebel* as

---

[8] "Our friendship wasn't easy, but I will miss it. If you're ending it today, it's probably because it was meant to end." And "Friendship can also become totalitarian; one must agree on everything or fight." Jean-Paul Sartre,

naive, apolitical, or sentimental. Camus, unwilling to retaliate in kind, let the rupture stand. At the time, most in the intellectual world thought that Camus took a philosophical beating from Sartre. And the split hurt him deeply. Not because Sartre was right, but because he had once believed their friendship was strong enough to contain disagreement.[9]

The Sartre-Camus split became emblematic: two public minds, once aligned in resistance, now diverging across a moral fault line. Sartre embraced the logic of *historical necessity*[10]. Camus rejected it. Sartre saw in revolution a tool for progress. Camus saw in it a threat to human dignity. The distinction was not merely intellectual. It was deeply ethical.

Camus did not argue that rebellion was wrong. He simply insisted that **means matter** — that the price of victory should not be paid in human souls. This placed him outside the dominant leftist current of his time. And it left him without a philosophical camp.

---

translation from *Les Temps Modernes*, July 1952, in the now-famous editorial "Reply to Camus," written largely by Francis Jeanson but approved and overseen by Sartre. This was a twenty page answer to the seventeen page reprint of Camus' letter, 'Lettre au Directeur au *Temps Modernes'* in response to the journal's criticism of *The Rebel*. Here Sartre unleashed a stream of personal accusations directed at Camus.

[9] Herbert Lottman, Albert Camus: A Biography (Doubleday, 1979), chapter 38 "Jonas". These pages detail Camus' profound belief in his friendship with Sartre, the shock and depth of the rupture, Sartre's political and personal attacks (including accusations of "moralism"), the intellectual reception of The Rebel, and Camus' refusal to retaliate. Lottman also records that the break left Camus deeply wounded for years, "as if the hurt would not go away," and that he suffered most from "lost illusions about the friendship of Sartre."

[10] "Historical necessity" refers to the belief — common in Hegelian, Marxist, and post-revolutionary thought — that history unfolds along a fixed trajectory toward justice or liberation. In this view, violent or repressive means are often justified by the assumption that they serve history's inevitable ends.

Chapter 3: Frozen in Time?

More importantly, it began to calcify the world's image of him. To his critics, he was now a *moralist without metaphysics* — too idealistic for revolution, too compromised for politics, too literary for philosophy.

But the truth was simpler:
Camus had not shifted. He remained committed to clarity, whatever it cost.
The world around him, increasingly uncomfortable with that clarity, shifted instead — seeking justification for a desired outcome, whatever the cost to truth.

The Nobel Moment

In 1957, Albert Camus received the Nobel Prize in Literature — at the age of forty-four. He was one of the youngest ever to receive the honor, and certainly one of the least comfortable with it.

The award was given "for his contribution to literature which illuminates the human conscience in our time." It was meant to affirm a life's work. But for Camus, it felt premature. The world was calling his voice complete. He knew it was still in motion.

He accepted the prize with grace but admitted privately that it felt more like a burden than a celebration. The pressure to now "speak for something" — to become the conscience of Europe, the oracle of postwar clarity — was precisely the kind of role he had spent his life resisting. Camus had no desire to become a monument. His voice had never come from authority, only from attentiveness.

His Nobel lecture was brief, human, and resolute. He spoke not of triumph, but of duty. He acknowledged that the writer is never truly free — he is bound to those who suffer, to those without a voice. But even here, Camus did not convert that duty into doctrine. He spoke as a man aware of his place in the world, but unwilling to claim more ground than he had earned.

In the years following the prize, he withdrew further from public discourse. He gave fewer interviews. He turned inward — to memory, to landscape, to childhood. It was not retreat. It was refinement. While others now quoted him as if he were finished, Camus continued writing — quietly, privately, and without resolution.

To many, the Nobel cemented Camus' place in the philosophical firmament. But it also froze him in time. From that point forward, he would often be read as if *The Rebel* were his final statement, as if *The Myth of Sisyphus* were his last word on existence. The subtle shift that was taking place — the warm, grounded tone of what was becoming The First Man — would go unheard until long after his death.

Camus had not declared himself finished.
The world, needing a statue, declared it for him.

Death and the Preservation Begins

On January 4th, 1960, Albert Camus died instantly in a car crash outside the town of Villeblevin. In the passenger seat was a manuscript — unfinished, handwritten, and stitched together from fragments. Thirty-four years later, it would be edited and published as *The First Man*.[11]

He had not intended it to be his final work.

---

[11] *The First Man*. Was posthumously published in French in 1994. The English version followed in 1995. The book provides a vivid account of his childhood in Belcourt and the profound influence of his teacher (Jacques Cormery, the protagonist, is a fictional stand-in for young Camus). The appendix of *The First Man* even includes the full text of Camus's 1957 letter to Louis Germain, a moving document of gratitude.

Chapter 3: Frozen in Time?

The suddenness of his death shocked the literary and philosophical world. He was 46 years old, perhaps at the height of his lucidity, but with no declared conclusion to his career, his thought, or his private inquiry. Yet the moment he died, a process began — not of mourning, but of *preservation.*

He was assigned a canon.
He was given a final shape.
The man who had spent his life resisting finalities became one.

Scholars returned to *The Myth of Sisyphus* and *The Rebel*, treating them as endpoints rather than thresholds. Obituaries praised his moral clarity but overlooked the questions he was still exploring. Posthumous commentary was careful, but also constricting. The trajectory of a life was now a summary. The arc of a voice was now a frame.

And for decades, *The First Man* remained unpublished.

Camus' daughter, Catherine, eventually brought it to light in 1994. The manuscript, incomplete and intimate, revealed something profound: Camus had not been circling back to his origins. He had been stepping forward into something softer, deeper, more integrated.

But by then, the cement had long since set.
Camus was the Absurdist.
Camus was the Rebel.
Camus was the philosopher who refused to be one.

The world had rendered Camus still.
But the manuscript he left behind tells a different story.

It would take time for readers — and some never would — to realize that the most important question about Camus was not *what he believed,* but *what he was becoming.*

Chapter 4: The Big Confusion: Camus was Not an Existentialist

Of all the ways Camus has been misunderstood, none has been more persistent than the label of "existentialist."

Even today, students, scholars, and critics routinely place him alongside Sartre, Kierkegaard, and Nietzsche — as though they were part of a single movement. The confusion is understandable. Camus wrote about the absurd, freedom, revolt, and suicide. He was praised early by existentialists. He was often photographed with them. But Camus never embraced the label — and neither did the ideas he lived by.

This chapter traces how the confusion began, why it persists, and why it matters. Not to defend Camus from miscategorization so much as to **liberate him from a frame he never accepted**. A frame that obscures what he was actually doing, and how far he had already moved beyond it.

The Absurd and Its Misunderstandings

Of all the words Camus gave the world, none has been more misunderstood than *the absurd*.

Later readers turned the absurd into the Absurd — a doctrine, a stance, a metaphysical category Camus never claimed.

It's the term that tethered him to the existentialists in the eyes of readers, critics, and even academics for decades. Sartre, Kierkegaard, Nietzsche, even Dostoevsky — all wrestled with the absurd in one form or another. And because *The Myth of Sisyphus* addressed it so directly, Camus was pulled into that lineage.

Part I: What Others Have Seen

But Camus meant something different.

For the existentialists, the absurd was a crisis to be confronted — a tension demanding resolution through meaning, freedom, or transcendence. In that view, existence comes first, and essence is built through the act of choosing.[12]

Camus saw none of this as necessary.

For him, the absurd was not a crisis but a fact — a limit to be named and accepted.

The entire debate about whether existence precedes essence was irrelevant to his perspective. Even Camus' notebooks underscore the point. In a 1953 entry, he dismisses the central metaphysical quarrel of his century with a single stroke:

> "Two common errors: existence precedes essence or essence existence. Both march and rise with the same step."[13]

To him, these were not rival doctrines. They were mirror-images — two philosophical constructions pretending to offer *foundations he simply did not require.* His thought moved elsewhere.

But the difference went beyond metaphysics. It was also a difference in attitude.

---

[12] Jean-Paul Sartre, "Existentialism Is a Humanism" (public lecture, Paris, 1945). The existentialist formula "existence precedes essence" is introduced and explained in this address. Sartre said: "If God does not exist, there is at least one being in whom existence precedes essence… a being who exists before he can be defined by any concept of it. That being is man." He further explained: "Man first exists: he materializes in the world, encounters himself, and only afterward defines himself."

[13] Camus, *Notebooks 1951–1959*, Ryan Bloom trans. (Ivan R. Dee, 2008), entry dated February 1953.
Written during the period when the rift with Sartre and the French Left had already taken full form.

Chapter 4: The Big Confusion: Camus was Not an Existentialist

He did not think the absurd could be overcome.
More importantly, he did not think it should be.

Where existentialists stared into the abyss and built meaning through choice, Camus stood beside the abyss, shrugged, and lived anyway — clear eyed and without illusion.

Existentialism's posture toward life was also different. In Sartre's *Nausea* (1938), the mood is unmistakable:

> "Every existing thing is born without reason, prolongs itself out of weakness, and dies by chance."

For Sartre, contingency is an affront. Being provokes revulsion. The fundamental experience of existence is a form of metaphysical sickness — a nausea that demands either explanation or escape through self-created meaning.

Camus never shared this temperament. Only four years later, in *The Myth of Sisyphus*, he arrives at a posture that could not be more different:

> "The struggle itself toward the heights is enough to fill a man's heart. One must imagine Sisyphus happy."

For Camus, the arbitrariness of the world is not a crisis. It is a condition of clarity. The world's indifference does not demand revolt through will; it invites lucidity through living. Where Sartre recoils, Camus breathes. Where Sartre sees weakness, Camus sees dignity. Where Sartre diagnoses sickness, Camus discovers a kind of austere warmth — a meaning that arises not from choice, but from presence.

This is not optimism. It is composure.
It is the difference between wrestling with existence and standing within it.
A contrast not merely of ideas, but of temperament — two attitudes toward life moving in opposite directions.

Camus was already moving toward something different than rebellion — *a kind of lucid indifference to everything in life that diminishes or undignifies us* — but that evolution would not be fully visible until the last years of his life.

Early Praise and Proximity to Sartre

Much of the confusion began with praise.

When *The Stranger* was published in 1942, Sartre reviewed it enthusiastically. He admired Camus' clarity, his detachment, and his treatment of moral ambiguity. The review helped elevate Camus into the existentialist spotlight — right alongside Sartre, Beauvoir, and Merleau-Ponty.

To make matters worse (or more tangled), Camus' first major essay, *The Myth of Sisyphus*, came out the same year. It dealt explicitly with absurdity, suicide, freedom, and revolt — themes that seemed to echo existentialism's deepest concerns.

So the label stuck.

Bookstores shelved him with existentialists.
Professors lumped him in with them.
Students wrote essays on "Camus as existentialist" for the next eighty years.

But even then, the cracks were forming.

Camus didn't speak of anguish.
He didn't build his identity around choice.
And he never reached for transcendence.

The Break: The Rebel and the Split

In 1951, Camus published *The Rebel*. It was his most ambitious work — an attempt to examine rebellion not just as a personal act, but as a historical and ethical force.

Chapter 4: The Big Confusion: Camus was Not an Existentialist

Sartre hated it.

So did most of the French left.

The book was a direct challenge to the ideological justifications that had come to dominate political life in the post-war period. Camus criticized **revolutionary violence, dialectical reasoning**, and the use of history as a moral excuse. He opposed **communism, totalitarianism**, and even **existentialist romanticism**, which he saw as too willing to trade clarity for cause.

The result: the public and painful rupture between Camus and Sartre.

But it wasn't just a political split.
It was a **philosophical divergence**.

Camus refused to align with movements.
He refused to grant historical inevitability the power to excuse cruelty.
He refused the premise that the future justified the present.

And in doing so, he placed himself **outside** existentialism — forever.

Camus' Own Denials — and Sartre's

Camus was explicit, spoken and written. Quietly, but consistently.
He said it in interviews. He said it to friends.
And while he never wrote that sentence in his notebooks, the notebooks contain something clearer: a running critique of existentialism itself. He mocked its jargon ("inexistential") [14],

---

[14] The term "inexistential" appears in Camus' Notebooks 1942–1951 as a parody of existentialist vocabulary, used to describe a "philosophy of exile" that substitutes negation for affirmation. See Albert Camus, *Notebooks 1942–*

Part I: What Others Have Seen

questioned its psychology ("judge-penitents") [15], rejected its metaphysics, and dismissed its posture as a form of theatrical self-incrimination. His public refusals were calm; his private reflections could be cutting. In either case, the distance was not tactical. It was total.

In a 1945 interview for *Les Nouvelles Littéraires*, Camus overtly stated: "No, I am not an existentialist. Sartre and I are always astonished to see our names associated. We are even thinking of publishing a little advertisement in which the undersigned affirm they have nothing in common and refuse to answer for the debts of the other."

Why the Confusion Still Persists

The confusion persists because the word *existentialist* has come to mean too many things — and mean them too vaguely.

For some, it means *rebellion*.
For others, *freedom*.
For still others, simply *cool French people in black turtlenecks*.

Camus fit the image.
But he rejected the idea.

He didn't build a system.[16]
He didn't seek transcendence.

1951, trans. Justin O'Brien (New York: Alfred A. Knopf, 1965), Sept. 15 1943 entry.
[15] Notebook entry, November 1954, cited in Herbert Lottman, *Albert Camus: A Biography*, chapter 35. The line appears only in the Pléiade edition of Camus' Carnets: "Existentialism: When they accuse themselves one can be sure that it is in order to crush others: judge-penitents."
[16] Camus remarked in a 1946 interview during his first trip to the United States, when pressed to define his philosophical position: "I'm too young to have a system." He added that his thought at the time consisted only of "doubts and uncertainties."
Source: Herbert Lottman, *Albert Camus: A Biography,* Chapter 29 ("New York").

Chapter 4: The Big Confusion: Camus was Not an Existentialist

He didn't make meaning.
He accepted the absurd and lived beside it.

In that sense, he was more ancient than modern.
More pagan than romantic.
More artist than philosopher.

Why It Matters

This isn't about labels. It's about motion.

Calling Camus an existentialist pins him in place — next to Sartre, under a heading he rejected, in a struggle he had already moved past.

He was not fighting for meaning.
He was not building a self.
He was not answering the absurd.

He was walking — lucidly, quietly, forward.
Not to conquer, but to endure without lying.

Camus said he was not an existentialist.
So we must, at the outset, take him at his word.

Let *his* be the last word on it.

Part II: What Camus Was Becoming

Chapter 5: The First Man's Turning

The first thing one notices when reading *The First Man* is the **tone**. It is not defiant. It is not diagnostic. It does not argue. It returns.

Where *The Myth of Sisyphus* confronts the void with clenched clarity, *The First Man* listens. It steps gently through dust, memory, and the fragile light of childhood. It does not build a system or propose a thesis. It opens a door.

Camus had not abandoned the absurd or the Rebel. He had not withdrawn from history or surrendered his convictions. But something had shifted — something in his center of gravity. The urgency to define had given way to a need to remember. The world no longer needed to be explained. It needed to be held.

There is little abstraction in *The First Man*. No declarations. No demands. Instead:

- a child walking barefoot through the streets of Algiers
- a mother who cannot read, but whose silence contains the weight of the world
- a father remembered only through the grave he left behind

And over all of it, a deepening humility. Not in the sense of defeat, but in the sense of rootedness.

Camus had always believed that thought must be grounded. But here, he is not grounding his ideas. He is grounding himself. He is placing his feet back into the earth of his origin — not to escape the world, but to walk forward with quieter purpose.

The manuscript is unfinished. The chapters trail off. Sentences stop mid-thought. But the direction is unmistakable. Camus is not circling back. He is stepping into a place he had not yet written from: **integration**. The rebel is still present. The absurd is still acknowledged. But now there is something else — something warmer, more lived, more human.

It is not a conclusion. It is a turning.

The shift in *The First Man* is not philosophical. It is physical. Sensory. Grounded.

There is no confrontation with the void, no rebellion against abstract injustice. There is a man at a gravesite, realizing that he is older than the father he barely knew. There is a mother, nearly silent, who becomes not an absence in his life but a *presence beyond words*. There is the sound of bare feet in dust. The weight of heat. The solidity of the world before thought.

These are not metaphors. Camus is no longer theorizing. He is **returning to what preceded all theory** — and allowing it to speak.

The mother, in particular, is a steady center. She cannot read. She does not speak much. But in her silence, there is no emptiness. There is power. Camus seems to recognize that whatever clarity he ever possessed began not with argument, but with her *unshakeable moral gravity*. She is not a concept. She is not a symbol. She is the untranslatable.

The father is a question he cannot answer. A man who died young, whose death Camus later learned was brutal. In one of the most human moments of the manuscript, Camus writes of standing at his father's grave and realizing, suddenly, that he had already outlived him. There is no philosophy here — only time. Only the fact that a life had been shorter than expected. That the world moves on without asking.

And yet, nothing in this manuscript is despairing.

Chapter 5: The First Man's Turning

What rises in its place is not system, but **acceptance**. Not the cold acceptance of existential resignation, but a kind of *warm neutrality* — a peace in simply being, even amidst questions without answers.

Camus is not withdrawing. He is integrating.

As we will examine more in Chapter 11, the voice in *The First Man* is no longer reaching forward in defiance of opposing forces. It is reaching downward, into the soil of memory and the grounded presence of things. It is an artful descent — not to escape meaning, but to live gently within its absence.

This is not reconciliation. It is not even recollection. It is *recognition*.

There is no moral program here. No manifesto. But there is motion — a turning of the body toward earth, the mind toward silence, and the heart toward something that feels like home.

What had begun many years before as a clear-eyed examination of existence had now turned into the ability to live at ease with it. The absurd was no longer something to answer. It had simply become a part of the natural world.

Chapter 6: Not Fighting the Absurd

In *The Myth of Sisyphus*, published in 1942, Camus writes that "there is but one truly serious philosophical problem, and that is suicide." It is a statement of enormous gravity — but also of enormous restraint. Camus is not making a declaration about death. He is framing a question about life: **is it worth continuing, when the world offers no ultimate answer?**

The absurd, for Camus, is born from the confrontation between two things:

- The human longing for meaning
- And the silence of the universe

The problem isn't that life is meaningless. The problem is that we *want* it to be otherwise.

And yet, even as he lays out this impasse, Camus refuses every solution that tries to leap over it — religion, ideology, even nihilism. He does not seek escape. He seeks *clarity*.

At the heart of *The Myth of Sisyphus* is not despair — it is defiance. Camus does not say, "all is meaningless." He says, "all is without final explanation — and yet, I live." The absurd man is not someone who gives in to futility. He is someone who lives *in full awareness of it*, and *chooses* to continue anyway.

But *The Myth of Sisyphus* is not warm. It is dry, rigorous, cerebral. It is a man setting down his terms and sharpening his tools. Camus is not at war with the absurd, but he is braced against it. He must *hold his shape* to survive it.

By the time of *The First Man*, something has changed.

Part II: What Camus Was Becoming

The absurd is still there — but it is no longer something to resist. It has lost its edge. It is not a condition to be confronted, but a texture to be lived with. Camus is no longer *facing off* against it. He is *walking beside* it.

In *The Myth of Sisyphus*, he imagines the condemned man happy as he descends the hill, only to once again take up his meaningless task — a symbol of conscious rebellion, and of choice to continue, even when no choice is offered. In *The First Man*, he no longer needs the symbol. He is simply walking. There is no hill. There is no heroism. There is only life, as it is.

This is not resignation. It is not even resolution. It is a kind of **ontological modesty** — a willingness to live without mastery. Camus was never seeking to solve the absurd, nor to overcome it. He simply refused to be dominated by it. His response was not a doctrine but a tone: lucidity without rebellion, presence without justification. He accepted the game without accepting its rules.

What is often described as a "softening" in Camus' later work is better understood as a deepening. The acceptance that critics see in *The First Man* was always latent — already visible in his earliest essays, though expressed then with the brightness of youth.

In *Nuptials at Tipasa* (1938), the younger Camus writes with an almost reckless clarity about joy, sunlight, and the body's agreement with the world:

> "There is no shame in being happy. But today the fool is king, and I call those who fear pleasure fools."

There is no metaphysics here. No leap, no denial, no argument. Just an insistence that the world is enough, and that refusing its moments of fullness is a kind of cowardice.

Chapter 6: Not Fighting the Absurd

Fourteen years later, in *Return to Tipasa* (1952), Camus comes back to the same landscape — changed, marked by war and grief, but still carrying a fidelity to the earth he knew as a young man. It is there he writes the line that has traveled farther than almost any other:

> "In the depths of winter, I finally learned that within me there lay an invincible summer."

This is not defiance. It is recognition — of hardship, yes, but also of the small reservoir of joy that survives despite it. The absurd has not vanished; it has simply lost its power to demand confrontation.

Around the same period, when asked in a 1956 interview whether Faulkner's faith contradicted his own "agnosticism," Camus resisted the label:

> "I don't believe in God, that's true. But I am not an atheist nonetheless."[17]

He refused belief and unbelief alike — not out of indifference, but out of a deeper refusal to let metaphysics dictate the terms of experience. The world, for Camus, needed no explanation. Its mystery was not a problem to solve.

What rises in these texts is not a theory but a posture: a way of living beside the absurd rather than against it. In *The First Man*, that posture becomes fully visible. Camus no longer writes to assert independence from the absurd by sheer will. He writes to inhabit a world where the absurd is simply one condition

---

[17] Albert Camus, "René Char," in *Lyrical and Critical Essays*, trans. Justin O'Brien (Vintage/Knopf), 1956.
First published in *Le Monde*, August 31, 1956.
Camus had already written the same line privately in his notebook of 1 November 1954: "Je ne crois pas à Dieu et je ne suis pas athée."

among others — present, acknowledged, and no longer disturbing.

And perhaps, after the long struggle, Camus' Sisyphus does not immediately descend again in defiance, nor climb again in repetition.
Perhaps there is a moment — brief but decisive — when he simply stands still: aware, lucid, and free.
Not in rebellion.
But in a refusal that no longer answers the absurd demand.

Ch. 7: The Rebel Who Had Already Won

When *The Rebel* appeared in 1951, it marked a turning point — not only in Camus' career, but in the intellectual climate of postwar Europe. Many read it as an attack on revolution itself, a repudiation of historical violence, or even—as some on the Left claimed — a betrayal of justice. Sartre and his circle denounced it as timid, apolitical, or bourgeois. These reactions fundamentally misunderstood what Camus was doing.

He was not proposing a political program, nor was he opposing any. **He was setting a limit.**

"I rebel — therefore we exist," Camus writes, in one of his most quoted and least understood lines.[18]

This is not a call to rise up, nor a license to destroy. It is a **recognition**—that the very act of refusing injustice affirms a common ground. The rebel begins alone but immediately implies others. The origin of rebellion is always individual — it begins with *I* — And in that moment, one discovers that one's protest reaches beyond oneself. The use of "we are" implies that rebellion, though personal, reveals a communal human bond — it affirms the existence of a moral "we" even when uttered alone. To draw a line is to declare that **something must not be crossed — not for anyone.**

---

[18] Camus' original phrasing in French is "Je me révolte, donc nous sommes," which literally translates to "I rebel, therefore we are." This is a deliberate inversion of Descartes' "I think, therefore I am," shifting the foundation of identity from individual cognition to shared moral refusal. The English translation "we exist" introduces ambiguity, as Camus was not making a metaphysical claim about being, but a relational one about dignity and solidarity.

This rebellion is not violent. It is not utopian. It does not seek victory.
It seeks to **preserve**.

Camus' rebel says *no* — not in nihilistic denial, but in **protective refusal**. He is not seeking to unmake the world. He is trying to keep it from unmaking what is most human. His "no" is not destructive. It is a boundary that creates space for something worth living for.

Camus describes the rebel as "a man who says no, but whose refusal does not imply a renunciation… a man who says yes from the moment he makes his first gesture of rebellion." [19] That "yes" is not an alternative program. It is a recommitment to meaning, not abstractly, but as a lived solidarity.

The rebel does not replace what he resists.
He holds his line, and says: **"This much, and no further."**

Camus' critics often mistook this restraint for weakness.
But it was not weakness.
It was proof that he had already won.

He was not arguing against systems because he wanted a better one.
He was standing outside the systems that were pressed to him because he no longer believed in their premise — that progress required blood, that history justified cruelty, that the end excused the means.

Camus' rebellion had nothing to do with spectacle. Unlike Nietzsche, he didn't shout. He didn't stage confrontation. He didn't gather crowds or claim to speak for them.

---

[19] Albert Camus, *The Rebel*, trans. Anthony Bower (Vintage International, 1991), Part One, "The Rebel".

Ch. 7: The Rebel Who Had Already Won

He simply lived in good faith — clear-eyed, unpersuaded, and morally intact. He refused the invitation to become an ideologue, even when the cost was exile from his intellectual peers. He was not against revolution because he feared it. He was against revolution because it **demanded too much from the future and too little from the present.**

He knew that the world was flawed beyond repair.
He also knew that dignity did not require repair — it required **integrity**.

And so he rebelled.
Not loudly. Not dramatically.
But consistently, and with full awareness.

His victory was not in changing the world, it was in remaining himself.
And from the moment he said "no," the victory was already complete.

Chapter 8: Freedom Without Excuse

Camus never believed that freedom was given. It could not be bestowed by society, by government, or even by reason. Freedom, for him, was always something internal — claimed, not inherited. What made his conception unique was that it came without metaphysical backing. He did not believe in fate. He did not believe in God — but neither did he believe in the necessity of God's absence. He rejected any sacred principle that secured freedom from above. He needed no metaphysical ground on which to stand, no system — whether religious or anti-religious — to justify his freedom.

Camus' refusal was undramatic. And yet — he believed in it fully.

This was his most radical clarity: he refused to excuse his freedom with any abstract rationale. He didn't need to. The act of being alive, awake, and aware was sufficient.

Where others grounded freedom in systems — moral law, historical dialectic, divine will — Camus grounded it in **lucidity**. Not in the right to do whatever one wants, but in the refusal to become what one is not.

He was not interested in permission.
He was interested in presence.

"Freedom is nothing else but a chance to be better," he wrote.[20] But he never defined what "better" meant. That was the point.

---

[20] Camus, *Resistance, Rebellion, and Death*, "In Defence of Freedom".

To live without excuse is not to live without ethics.
It is to live without illusion—without leaning on reasons that justify compromise.

Camus' kind of freedom is not assertive. It's not a demand. It's not about power.
It's about **poise** — a way of standing in the world that answers to nothing but itself.

In this sense, Camus redefined the moral landscape.

One does not need to believe in ultimate meaning in order to act meaningfully.
One does not need to explain one's choices in order to choose well.
One does not need to win by any rules but one's own, if even that.

In *The First Man*, Camus does not speak of freedom. He enacts it.
There are no declarations. No manifestos.
Just a man walking through his past, with no one to impress and nothing to prove.
He does not justify his decisions.
He does not explain his values.
He simply **lives them** — with clarity, with care, and without apology.

The main character, Jacques Cormery, is not heroic. He is not defiant.
But he moves through the world with an awareness that nothing is owed, and nothing is promised — and yet everything is worth attending to.

His mother, barely literate, becomes a figure of immense weight — not because of what she says, but because of how she endures. She does not claim freedom. She does not fight

Chapter 8: Freedom Without Excuse

for it. She simply lives—**without self-pity, without justification**, and with a kind of quiet exactness that Camus understood as deeper than rhetoric.

This is the freedom Camus ultimately arrived at — not the freedom to act, but the freedom **to stand unguarded**, fully aware, and free of the need for explanation.

It is not the kind of freedom that demands recognition.
It is the kind of freedom that survives without it.

Camus never asked permission to exist.

He did not ask the world to explain itself.
He did not wait for the universe to justify his place in it.
He did not need a system to validate his freedom.

He simply stood.
Lucid. Present. Undeceived.
And that was enough.

Chapter 9: The Artist's Mindset

Camus never called himself a philosopher. He preferred — if anything — to be known as a writer. But the word he returned to most was *artist*.

This was not modesty. It was clarity.

Philosophers, he believed, sought systems. They constructed meanings, then defended them. Artists, by contrast, revealed what was already there — without judgment, without demand, without flinching. If the philosopher builds, the artist witnesses.

And for Camus, witnessing was the highest form of integrity. "A man's work," he wrote, "is nothing but this slow trek to rediscover, through the detours of art, those two or three great and simple images in whose presence his heart first opened." [21]

These lines do more than describe the artist's path. They reveal his own. Camus was not changing course in his later work; he was completing it. What looks like evolution is, in truth, a deepening — different approaches to the same original clarity. The images he mentions are not memories. They are foundations. And "in whose presence" was not a casual phrase. These images carried the weight that others reserve for the divine — not supernatural, but supreme in his inner life.

Everything that matters in Camus — lucidity, presence, freedom without excuse, the refusal to lie, the dignity of standing where one stands — is simply a different face of that same *first* vision. His work moves forward, but always toward the beginning. And *The First Man* is its last return.

---

[21] Camus, "The Wrong Side and the Wright Side", Preface, in *Lyrical and Critical Essays*, trans. Justin O'Brien.

Part II: What Camus Was Becoming

This is not a blueprint. It's a way of walking.
A return to origin, not escape.
A form of clarity that does not require conquest.

Where others tried to explain the world, Camus tried to hold it still long enough to see it clearly.

This is why *The First Man* matters — not only as a memoir or a novel, but as a demonstration of the artist's mind in motion. There is no thesis in that book. There is only return — to soil, to silence, to sunlight, to sorrow. Not to analyze. Not to resolve. But to reveal.

In that final work, Camus does not abstract the human experience.
He lets it be common.

And in doing so, he shows that art is not a reaction to suffering.
It is a refusal to lie about what suffering is.

The artist does not deny the absurd.
He does not resolve it.
He simply keeps his eyes open — and paints what he sees.

For Camus, language was not a tool of persuasion. It was a form of presence.

He distrusted rhetoric. He distrusted even precision when it became a substitute for truth. He was not interested in argument. He was interested in tone — in the texture of honesty as it passed through a voice that refused to distort.

Style, for Camus, was the soul's honesty.

That is why Camus' writing — whether in novels, essays, or notebooks — carries such restraint. Not because he lacked

Chapter 9: The Artist's Mindset

passion, but because he feared the damage that overstatement could do to truth.

He chose words the way an artist chooses light.
Not to decorate.
To reveal.

Where many philosophers aimed for finality, Camus chose exactness without excess.
He allowed for silence.
He let a sentence stand when others would explain it twice.
He preferred a paragraph that suggested tension to one that claimed to resolve it.

This is not minimalism.
This is discipline born of moral caution.

Camus understood that the power of language was also its danger. It could be used to justify — to abstract violence, to mask ideology, to make lies sound like reason. He had seen it in war. He had seen it in revolution. And so he stepped back, writing always with a sense of responsibility not to say more than what was true.

That is what made him an artist.
Not that he created symbols.
But that he refused to falsify the world in order to explain it.

In the end, Camus was not trying to express a philosophy.
He was becoming a presence.

He no longer needed to define freedom, or rebellion, or even the absurd.
He had already lived them — and let them fall away.

Part II: What Camus Was Becoming

What remained was something more whole than theory, more enduring than resistance:

> a man who wrote what he saw, lived what he wrote, and asked nothing more from the world than the right to meet it with his eyes open.

Ch. 10: Sisyphus Walks Down the Hill

In *The Myth of Sisyphus*, Camus leaves us with the image of the condemned man walking down the slope — having pushed his stone once more to the summit, fully aware of the cycle, and yet with a contentment that he lacked previously..

It was an image of rebellion, of lucid repetition, of a man who affirms his fate not by escaping it, but by refusing to be broken by it.

But perhaps that was never the end of the story.

Perhaps there comes a moment—after many descents, after many moments of strength — when Sisyphus no longer returns to the stone.
Not out of defiance. Not out of despair.
But because he no longer accepts the premise of the sentence. And because there is no longer any need to demonstrate that "he is stronger than his rock".[22]
Nothing to prove. Nothing to win.

The absurd has not vanished.
It is still present, like heat, like silence.
But it no longer demands a response.

Sisyphus walks down the hill.
But he does not return.
He simply continues — aware, lucid, and free.

---

[22] *The Myth of Sisyphus*, translated by Justin O'Brien, published in 1955 by Vintage Books. This quote is taken from the essay within the book by the same title.

Part III: Beyond the Last Page

Chapter 11: What We Know: The Direction Camus Was Moving

A man in motion.

By the time of his death in January 1960, Camus was no longer the man who had written *The Myth of Sisyphus* (1942), nor even the embattled author of *The Rebel* (1951). He had begun to shift — not in contradiction to his earlier works, but in calm evolution beyond them. Much of this book has hinted at that motion; this chapter finally substantiates it. Here we set aside mythmaking and retrospective projection to ask a simpler and more sober question: what do we actually know about the direction Camus was moving? Not what he might have become, but what he had already become by the end of his life. We turn to the final manuscripts, the notebooks, and the spoken fragments he left behind — not for grand revelation, but for the lived momentum, the unmistakable tilt of his spirit in its final seasons.

The First Man: Tone and Trajectory

Camus' final manuscript, *The First Man*, left unfinished at his death and published posthumously by his daughter Catherine, reveals a tonal transformation. In private notes and late interviews, Camus made clear that this book was to begin a new cycle in his work — more personal, more embodied, and, as Catherine Camus later confirmed, the most important project of his life. [23] Gone is the pointed moral rhetoric of *The Rebel*,

---

[23] Camus envisioned The First Man as the beginning of a new "cycle of love" to complement his earlier cycles on the absurd and rebellion, as noted

Part III: Beyond the Last Page

replaced by a warmer, more grounded mode of reflection. The text is rooted in physical place — Algeria, childhood, Mediterranean light. It is less concerned with asserting a position and more committed to evoking a presence.

The narrative is not structured by argument but by return: to memory, to the sensory world, to the fragments that shaped a life. The prose breathes differently. There is less strain. Less defense. Even when confronting loss, Camus writes with a spaciousness, an unguarded touch that suggests not resignation but *recognition*.

If this language feels familiar, it should. This book returns to *recognition* again and again, just as Camus returned to the sun— not to repeat a thought, but to approach it from a clearer angle each time. His late work is not a break from the past, but a deeper turn toward what had always been there.

The First Man was not only a novel. It was an act of love and recovery — an attempt to reunite his fragmented past with the voice of a father he never knew and a mother who had never spoken much. It was not written to persuade. It was written to listen.

> *This is not reconciliation. It is not even recollection. It is recognition.*

This phrase might best capture the tonal gesture of *The First Man*. An *untroubled* acceptance, not forced into synthesis, but allowed to stand as it is — one of the final insights in *The First*

---

in his late notebooks. His daughter, Catherine Camus, later affirmed that he considered it the most important and personal work of his life. Biographer Olivier Todd describes this project as a tonal and philosophical shift — a turn from polemic toward rooted presence, away from public confrontation and into interiority. In a letter to actress Catherine Sellers written shortly before his death, Camus expressed his deep concern that he would not live to complete the novel — an urgency that affirms its emotional and existential weight.

Chapter 11: What We Know: The Direction Camus Was Moving

Man — serves not as a thesis, but as a closing gesture of motion. Camus is no longer climbing the hill. He is looking at the hill from a distance, and perhaps, at last, forgiving it, and its boulder, for being there.

Notebooks and Interviews: What Remains Unwritten

Camus' notebooks from the mid-1950s offer an even clearer glimpse of the direction he intended for his unwritten final cycle. After the cycles of the absurd and revolt, he envisioned a third movement anchored in the figure of **Némésis** — not as vengeance, but as the **ancient guardian of measure, balance, and the rightful limits of the human heart**. In a 1953 notebook entry, he writes that love itself carries an unavoidable guilt, that true love must be chosen alone, and that one must bear its consequences without the alibis of ideology or collective morality.[24] This is not sentiment; it is a rigorous ethics of tenderness. It shows the new ground he was approaching: a world where love, responsibility, and measure were no longer opposites but facets of the same truth. Editorial notes to *The First Man* confirm that Camus intended this book to inaugurate that final cycle — centered on Némésis and shaped around the theme of love.[25]

The notes contain fewer polemics and more fragments of observation: birdsong, silence, olive trees. He was thinking about children, about education, about return. There is a

---

[24] Albert Camus, *Carnets (Tome 3): mars 1951–décembre 1959* (Paris: Gallimard), 89.
The entry, dated 15 février 1953, appears under the heading "Némésis" and includes Camus' reflections on love, guilt, solitude, and responsibility: « Il arrive que l'amour tue… » etc.
[25] Raymond Gay-Crosier, note 47 to *Albert Camus, Carnets III: mars 1951–décembre 1959* (Paris: Gallimard), 339.
Gay-Crosier notes: « Nous savons qu'après le cycle de l'absurde et celui de la révolte Camus avait envisagé un temps de consacrer un cycle à Némésis autour du thème de l'amour auquel devait appartenir Le Premier Homme. »

Part III: Beyond the Last Page

marked re-centering of the world through the body and through time, rather than through metaphysical tension.

He was not seeking new terrain to conquer. He was seeking old ground to re-enter — to feel the soil and the dust beneath his own memory.

In interviews from 1957 to 1959, Camus sounded fatigued by public life. He did not attack his critics; he simply refused to meet them where they stood. In these years, Camus rejected attempts to cast him as a leader or a spokesman. The next stage of his work, he wrote in his notebooks, would be the moment when he could finally "speak in my own name".[26]

This was not detachment. It was a redirection of energy — from polemic to precision, from rhetoric to reality.

The Silences and the Softening

Perhaps more revealing than what Camus said is what he stopped saying. *The Rebel* was filled with friction. *The First Man* is filled with light. The notebooks thin out. The declarations fade. What emerges is not a retreat, but a kind of elemental composure.

He had not ceased working — but he had withdrawn from public debates. The Cold War. The Algerian conflict. The existential battles of the Left. He does not renounce his ideas, but he sheds the role of prophet. His guidance now takes the form of encouraging others to guide themselves.

He was no longer searching for a new system. He was no longer warding off bad faith. He was simply living with what

---

[26] Albert Camus, *Notebooks 1942–1951*, trans. Justin O'Brien (New York: Alfred A. Knopf, 1965), Notebook VI ("April 1948 – March 1951").

Chapter 11: What We Know: The Direction Camus Was Moving

had always been there. The dust. The heat. The impenetrable quiet of his mother. The unwavering dignity of the poor.

In this silence, Camus seemed to be discovering not an answer, but a rhythm.

From Absurd to Accepted: His Changing Relationship with the Absurd

Camus' early writings wrestled with the absurd. They named it, resisted it, shaped identities around it. But by the end, there was no need to resist. The absurd had not disappeared. It had simply stopped being a problem.

He no longer presented Sisyphus as a symbol of rebellion. He no longer needed to. The absurd had become, in his late work, something closer to atmospheric: present, defining, but no longer oppressive. Like weather. Like gravity. Like stone.

Camus accepts his past positions — on the absurd, on rebellion — but allows that they are incomplete. He does not apologize. But he no longer explains.

To live beside it was enough. No revolt required.

Where the Arc Was Pointing

Camus was not abandoning the past, or even the toils of *his* rock. He was absorbing it. The movement was not toward a new doctrine or a final synthesis. It was toward presence. He had already moved beyond argument. He was arriving, finally, at attention.

If there is a shape to his last phase, it is not ascent. It is settling. Not resignation, but deepening. A moral topography. A homecoming. A life that no longer needed to justify itself. The question of meaning — so urgent in his early work — no longer pressed against him. He did not resolve it. He simply stopped requiring it. The absence of ultimate meaning no longer threatened dignity or demanded rebellion. It had become, like the absurd itself, part of the atmosphere: not something to confront, but something to breathe through. What mattered was not whether life had meaning, but whether one could live attentively without needing it to.

He no longer needed certainty to feel at peace. The drive to define had softened into the capacity to notice. Where he once sought clarity as a tool of defense, it now emerged as a quality of stillness — a form of inner alignment rather than a position to hold.

It has been said that hate is the opposite of love. It is not. Hate is still entanglement. The true opposite is indifference — the absence of the hook.

In his early works Camus recognized a kind of intellectual indifference to the absurd: the refusal to be deceived by metaphysics or consoled by meaning. In *The First Man*, the register changes. The indifference becomes embodied, no longer an idea but a way of standing in the world. It is indifference not to life, but to all that diminishes it. Freed from the need to oppose the absurd, he could turn toward love, and beauty, and sun.[27]

This is not speculation. It is observation. These were the steps he had already taken. And now, beyond the last page, we are invited to take the next ones.

---

[27] See Appendix A for an expanded analysis of Camus' late-stage transition from intellectual clarity to lived presence.

Chapter 12: Living Without the Leap

What kind of life becomes possible when one no longer searches for ultimate answers?
When the leap is neither rejected nor feared — simply no longer needed?

By the end of his life, Camus no longer argued against belief. He had simply outgrown the posture of confrontation.

In *The Myth of Sisyphus*, the absurd required a decision. Suicide or revolt. Leap or lucidity.
But in *The First Man*, there is no such ultimatum.
There is only presence. Memory. The sound of footsteps through dust. A mother who says little, and understands everything.

Camus had not changed his conclusions. But he had changed his stance.
What began in rebellion now lived in restraint.
What began in opposition now lived in awareness.

From Argument to Poise

To live without the leap is not to live in despair.
It is to stop demanding an answer that never arrives.

It is not a denial of meaning. It is a refusal to be governed by the need for one.

Camus was not cold in this posture. He was warmer than ever. More rooted. More attentive.

He had never lived by a system.
What changed was that he no longer needed to explain why.

Part III: Beyond the Last Page

Camus' rejection of the need for a system is not nihilism. It led to the opposite.
It is a life cleared of illusion — and therefore, free to notice what remains:

- The weight of a hand on a shoulder.
- The silence of a room after someone has left it.
- The scent of heat rising from the stones at Tipasa.

There is no metaphysical lift here. No arc to the heavens. Only the rhythm of a life walked in full view of its limits.

The End of Justification

To live without the leap is to stop justifying one's freedom.

Not because freedom doesn't matter — but because it no longer needs to be explained.

In this light, Camus' late ethic emerges:
An ethic without commandments.
A clarity without conquest.
A freedom not granted, nor is it taken, but simply lived.

A Rhythm, Not a Conclusion

The Camus of the first two cycles lived under the pressure of metaphysical questions: suicide, meaning, rebellion, justice, the leap.
The Camus of the third did not. Those questions no longer needed answers. They no longer even needed to be asked.
He was free of them.

Chapter 12: Living Without the Leap

The old pressures belonged to the first Camus — the Camus of the absurd and of revolt.
They demanded answers:
- Must one choose suicide or endurance?
- Must one justify a life lived without transcendence?
- Must one fight against meaninglessness?
- Must one decide whether murder or justice can be grounded?
- Must one reject the leap or explain why one has not taken it?

All of these questions shaped the first two cycles.
None of them shaped the last.

My work during these first two cycles: persons without lies, hence not real. They are not of this world. This is probably why up to now I am not a novelist in the usual sense. But rather an artist who creates myths to fit his passion and his anguis. This is also why the presons who have meant much to me in this world are always those who had the force and exclusiveness of thos myths.[28]

In the Camus of *The First Man*, he loosened his grip on anguish. There were no longer problems to resolve, positions to defend, or arguments to complete. They no longer demanded answers — or even attention. The absurd had become part of the weather: shaping the terrain, yes, but no longer shaping him. The need for a leap had faded because the need for justification itself had fallen away.

This is what it means to live without the leap:
not nihilism, not resignation, but a life not only no longer governed by metaphysical demands.
But also a life cleared of explanation.

---

[28] Albert Camus, *Notebooks 1942–1951*, trans. Justin O'Brien (New York: Alfred A. Knopf, 1965), Notebook VI, May 27 1950 entry.

Part III: Beyond the Last Page

A life lived in its own rhythm — walking, noticing, caring, touching, being — without the pressure to justify itself against the universe.

What mattered now was the walk itself.
The rhythm of care. The refusal to pretend.
The ability to stand lucid in the midst of impermanence — and smile, not because life made sense, but because it was still worth touching.

Camus did not need to leap.
He had arrived.

Chapter 13: The Quiet Middle

In a world that demands allegiance to one extreme or the other, Camus stood still.
Not because he lacked conviction, but because he refused to lie.

Camus rejected the trap that caught nearly every major thinker of his century — and most of the centuries before it: the desire to turn insight into system.

He did not want a doctrine. He wanted clarity.

Where others drew diagrams, Camus drew breath. Where others codified, he listened. He did not need a glossary to explain the human condition. He had lived it. Poverty. War. Injustice. Love. Silence. Death. These were not ideas to be defined. They were facts to be faced.

Systematization, for Camus, was not philosophy. It was ego — the desire to assert one's intellect over the mess of existence. He saw how the great "isms" of his time used definitions to consolidate control. How systems could excuse cruelty in the name of order. How abstractions could overwrite the body.

He refused it all. Not by critique, but by stance.

Between the Poles

Camus stood in the quiet middle — not because he lacked a position, but because he had seen what happened to those who let their positions harden into ideologies. The extremes offered false clarity: purity through negation, righteousness through violence, meaning through suffering.

Part III: Beyond the Last Page

He chose none of these.

- He would not become a nihilist.
- He would not become a utopian.
- He would not sign the dotted line for any system that demanded loyalty above lucidity.

Instead, he practiced a moral poise — an ethic of attention rather than assertion. He judged realities, not theories. Acts, not slogans.

Where others yelled, Camus watched. Where others divided the world, Camus stood between the lines.

The Middle Is Not the Center

To be clear: Camus was not a moderate in the sense of seeking compromise. He was not trying to "balance" views. He was not timid.

He had sharp views on justice, on dignity, on violence. But he refused to express them through allegiance. He rejected the machinery of groupthink. He refused to become a brand.

The quiet middle is not the place of comfort. It is the place of tension.

To stand there is to feel pulled from both sides — sometimes welcomed by neither. To remain there is to choose clarity over popularity. To speak from there is to risk being misunderstood by those who need a flag to follow.

Camus bore that risk. Not dramatically. These conflicts did grieve him — and the notebooks reveal how deeply they weighed on him. But the sorrow never hardened into self-pity.

Chapter 13: The Quiet Middle

Like his lifelong illness, it was something inextractable from living his life in good faith — to himself, and with lucidity.

Staying Big

While others narrowed their work into tightly defined systems, Camus stayed big.

He did not reduce the absurd to a formula.
He did not reduce freedom to a slogan.
He did not reduce revolt to a prescription.

He stayed human.

He wrote in wide spaces — wind, sand, silence. He left room for contradiction. For adjustment. For change.

He never claimed to have the last word. Only the next breath.

A Position Without a Program

The quiet middle is not indecision. It is refusal. Refusal to become a spokesman. Refusal to surrender subtlety. Refusal to choose sides when both are lying.

Camus was not without values. He had them in abundance.

But they were lived, not labeled. Felt, not fixed. His ethics were situational — not in the sense of being weak, but in the sense of being awake.

He did not look for moral formulas. He looked at people. And when he spoke, it was not from a podium. It was from the center of his own presence.

This is what allowed him to remain lucid when others went blind with certainty. This is why his work still breathes.

Part III: Beyond the Last Page

Because he never tried to explain everything. He only tried to see clearly.

And perhaps, that is the most radical position of all.

Chapter 14: Refusal Without Rage

Camus was not a man of spectacle. His defiance made no noise.

His was not the posture of the protestor, but the stance of the steady. He refused, but he did not shout. He withheld, but he did not accuse. Where others threw stones at the systems they opposed, Camus simply stepped aside. He declined to participate in the lie — and that, for him, was enough.

This refusal was not passive. It was principled. It was not born of weakness, but of **boundary**.

Camus drew his line, then honored it. That line was never abstract. It was drawn in lived moments, in moral specifics, in silence when others demanded slogans.

The Strength of the Withheld

To refuse without rage is not to surrender passion — it is to discipline it. Rage devours clarity. Camus knew that. He had seen how movements driven by purity of anger often turned into engines of cruelty.

He had no interest in that transformation.

So he stepped back. Not in retreat, but in composure. His refusal was not a collapse. It was a stance.

He believed in justice. But not vengeance. He believed in freedom. But not domination. He believed in clarity. But not control.

Part III: Beyond the Last Page

Where others stormed the gates, Camus sat by the wall and watched. Not out of apathy — but because he refused to let injustice turn him into its mirror.

A Line That Does Not Shout

Camus' ethic of refusal was defined not by noise, but by **lucid boundaries**. He would not write slogans. He would not praise murderers. He would not excuse cruelty in the name of the future.

And so he was called a coward. A traitor. An indecisive man.

But the truth was simpler: he had drawn his line earlier than most. And he did not move it. Not even when it cost him friends, reputation, readers, or approval.

And yet, the line was not fixed. Though inwardly wounded, Camus was still moving — still evolving. Not in contradiction, but in refinement. His boundaries toward others remained firm, but his boundaries within himself softened. He was no longer guarding his position. He was walking toward something quieter. Not to redraw the line, but to deepen it.

Dignity Without Victory

Camus was not trying to win. That was his heresy.

He refused to treat life as a contest. His clarity was not a weapon. His freedom was not a campaign. He simply stood where he believed he must stand.

And when others demanded an explanation, he did not perform one.

He did not dress his defiance in righteousness. He did not moralize his restraint. He simply lived it.

Chapter 14: Refusal Without Rage

He wrote without applause. He worked without platform. He lived as though the posture of truth was reward enough.

The Elegance of Refusal

This is what gives Camus his gravity. His resistance was not flamboyant. It did not need an audience. It was quiet. Precise. Final.

He did not burn bridges. He simply stopped walking toward them.

And when the noise around him rose, he did not shout back. He returned to the sea. To silence. To the clear morning air of Tipasa.

Not to escape, but to remain unbroken.

This is how a man refuses without rage. This is how one lives with clean hands in a dirty time.

Not by winning or yelling, nor even by walking away — but by remaining present, without apology, and continuing to live.

This is where Camus stood in his final years — in stillness. He had already refused all the false choices. What remained was not a position to defend, but a presence to inhabit.

This is how he met the world: not with accusation or certainty, but with a refusal to become what he opposed.

And that, more than argument, was the gesture that carried him beyond the last page.

Chapter 15: Presence, Not Performance

Camus did not display his convictions. He lived them.

In a time of posturing, Camus remained exact. His clarity did not perform. His ethics did not demand recognition. He stood where he stood — not to be seen, but because it was the only honest place he could stand.

There is a kind of presence that asks nothing from the world. It does not seek applause. It does not explain itself. It does not cultivate the image of integrity — it simply moves with it. That is the kind of presence Camus embodied.

The Refusal to Pose

Camus refused to become an icon. Not because he feared the attention, but because he saw how quickly symbols become false. Once a person becomes a symbol, others start to speak for them. Their meaning gets diluted, then inverted. Their clarity is replaced by interpretation, their presence by projection.

Camus resisted that.

He did not campaign for a moral position. He did not try to sculpt his reputation. Even at the height of his fame, he seemed to treat recognition as a byproduct — never as a goal.

He had no interest in shaping history's opinion. He was interested in living truthfully now.

Part III: Beyond the Last Page

The Weight of the Unspoken

There is a dignity in restraint. In not explaining yourself. In refusing to let others' noise define your tone. Camus carried this restraint without wavering.

He never denied the pressures of his time. But he refused to answer them with spectacle. He offered no manifestos. No grand gestures. He wrote, he walked, he endured.

Where Sartre demanded attention, Camus turned toward silence. Where others competed for moral terrain, Camus remained grounded in what he could see and touch. He did not perform clarity. He lived with it.

The Undivided Life

Camus did not separate his life from his values. He did not play a public role and then retreat to a private contradiction. He aligned his work, his speech, and his silences.

This did not make him flawless. It made him honest.

He did not claim consistency. But he remained coherent.

He did not claim virtue. But he refused to lie.

He lived the life he wrote about, even when that life became difficult to defend. Even when it left him alone. Even when others called him indecisive, or soft, or weak.

But Camus was not soft. He was grounded. He was not indecisive. He was discerning. He was not weak. He simply did not need to be loud.

Why He Still Speaks

In an age that merely repeats what every age before it has known — where performance saturates politics, art, and even

Chapter 15: Presence, Not Performance

ethics — Camus remains vital because he shows us another way: to live in good faith to the self, not as display, but as a discipline of attention.

He didn't try to matter. He tried to be exact.

He never asked to be followed. He simply walked.

And for those willing to stop performing long enough to pay attention, his presence is still here.

Quiet. Clear. Undeceived.

He left no system. No map. No resolution.
What he offered was something rarer: a posture from which one could walk forward.

We have now followed that posture to the last page he wrote. What remains is not to explain him further, but to consider what such clarity allows.

If Camus refused every system, where does that refusal lead us?

That is the question we now turn to. Not what Camus meant — but what he made possible.

Part IV: Camus Beyond the Systems

Chapter 16: Introductory

Camus did not found a school. He did not leave a system. He left a rhythm.

Throughout this book, we have followed Camus — not as a philosopher of definitions, but as a man in motion. We have resisted the temptation to extract a doctrine from his life. He offered none. What he gave us instead was a kind of posture: a stance of clarity, refusal, and presence.

And yet, that posture did not emerge in a vacuum. Camus read deeply. He responded to the thinkers of his time and to those who came before him. His silence toward systems was not born of ignorance. It was born of discernment.

Camus did not systematize. But he stood in relation to systems.

He admired the discipline of the Stoics, but could not join their apathy. He shared the questions of the Existentialists, but not their despair. He named the absurd, but refused to let it become a doctrine. Others would later call it *Absurdism* — he never did. He respected certain spiritual traditions, but never surrendered to mysticism.

This final section explores those relationships — not to compare, but to clarify. Not to gather Camus into a lineage, but to highlight the space he chose to inhabit. And just as importantly, the spaces he refused. Camus cannot be understood by where others placed him. He is understood only by the boundaries he would not cross — the systems he would not enter, the explanations he would not accept, the comforts he would not claim. What remains is the clearing he made for himself.

First off, Camus did not stand within any system, but he stood near many. His distances were deliberate; his proximities were cautious. To trace these edges is not to assign him a doctrine, but to see better the rhythm he chose to live by.

We do so not by surveying every philosopher or tradition, but by moving through the most relevant systems of thought, both Western and Eastern. In each case, we ask:

- What does the system seek?
- Where does Camus align?
- Where does he diverge?
- What does his refusal illuminate?

This is not an exhaustive comparison. To attempt one here would be a fool's errand anyway — clouding rather than clarifying. This is a conversation across boundaries.

We begin not with metaphysics or mysticism, but with the ground beneath Camus' feet: the Western philosophical tradition that shaped the intellectual world he both inherited — and refused.

Systems and Distinctions

To place Camus among the systems, we must first understand what we mean by "system".

Before stepping into comparisons, a clarification is needed — not just for Camus, but for anyone attempting to navigate the philosophical landscape.

Chapter 16: Introductory

Western philosophy and Eastern thought are often spoken of in the same breath, but they do not grow from the same root. Their goals, their methods, and even their assumptions about what knowledge is — differ.

To understand Camus' position in relation to these traditions, we must first distinguish the traditions themselves.

Philosophy as a Western Discipline

Philosophy, in the classical sense, is a **Western invention** — formalized in ancient Greece and rooted in **three primary domains**:

1. **Epistemology** – The study of knowledge. What do we know? How do we know it?

2. **Ethics** – The conduct of one's life. How should we live?

3. **Politics** – Governance. How should society be ordered?

These categories form the basis of most Western philosophical systems, from Plato and Aristotle to Kant, Hegel, and Sartre. Western philosophy, or simply philosophy, is primarily **analytical**: it dissects, defines, and systematizes. Its method is dialectical — built on debate, opposition, and resolution. It seeks **clarity through coherence**.

Camus was shaped by this world — and eventually resisted it.

He was fluent in the tradition, but wary of its hunger for totalizing explanations. His clarity was not built from systems. It was earned through confrontation — with war, with suffering, with the absence of metaphysical grounding. He understood the philosophical imperative to define, but by the end of his life, he had begun to live in a way that refused the need for finality.

Eastern Thought: Living Holistically

By contrast, Eastern traditions — Taoism, Buddhism, Confucianism, Vedanta — do not begin with categorization. They begin with **experience**. Their purpose is not to define the world, but to **inhabit it well**.

Eastern thought tends to:

- Prioritize **integration over analysis**
- Seek **harmony** rather than certainty
- Embrace **paradox** rather than eliminate it
- Value **embodied presence** over discursive clarity

While philosophy of the West often asks, "What is truth?", Eastern thought more often asks, "How shall I live?"

To many in the East, the very act of systematizing wisdom turns it into something else — less alive, less human. And so, the most profound teachings often arrive in metaphor, silence, or gesture.

This does not make Eastern traditions irrational or anti-intellectual. It makes them **relational**. Their logic is circular, not linear. Their goal is **poise**, not proof.

Why This Matters for Camus

Camus did not belong to the East. Yet, looking across the arc of his life, we can see that he progressively stepped away from the Western compulsion to define. In his third cycle, he was no longer seeking argumentative victory. He was seeking presence

Chapter 16: Introductory

— a life that did not need to be justified in order to be lived well.

In this way, Camus stands at a threshold:

- Formed by the West
- Tempered by suffering
- And moving toward a stance that begins to echo the East, without ever trying to imitate it.

This is why comparing Camus to Stoicism, Existentialism, or Taoism is not an attempt to "place" him, but to **clarify his distance**—and to highlight the singular, sovereign path he chose.

It is not a path through systems. It is a rhythm that passes between them.

Chapter 17: Western Philosophical Systems

Camus stood within the Western tradition—but always at an angle to it.

The Western philosophical lineage shaped the intellectual world Camus inherited. He knew its language. He read its canonical works. He taught philosophy. But he never seemed to be at home within its systems.

In this chapter, we walk briefly through a few of the systems that most closely surrounded Camus — those that critics often attempt to link him with, or against. Our purpose is not to judge these systems, but to observe how Camus approached their terrain — and ultimately, how he refused to stay within their boundaries.

We begin with the oldest voice of composure in the West:

To understand where he stood at the end — and where he was likely headed — we begin not with his contemporaries, but with the older soil they all shared.

The Pre-Socratics – Origin Without System

Before philosophy became a discipline, it was a kind of seeing. The early Greek thinkers — Heraclitus, Anaximander, Parmenides, Pythagoras — wrote in fragments, not treatises. They sought to name the patterns of the world, not yet to control them. Their logic was poetic, elemental, and intuitive.

Camus admired this spirit. In Heraclitus he found a world of tension and becoming. In Anaximander, a vision of existence that is bounded by justice, even among the stars. He, too, believed in limits — not as restriction, but as clarity.

But Camus did not share their metaphysical drive. He had no interest in first causes or cosmological models. The absurd, for him, is not something to solve. It is something to see. The Pre-Socratics gestured toward a hidden order. Camus faced the silence.

If he carried anything from them, it was the stance: **humble, attentive, unresolved.**

Socrates, Plato, Aristotle – The Turn Toward Structure

Socrates stood at the pivot. His method was not to teach, but to question. He refused to lie. He refused to flatter. He died rather than speak against his conscience.

Camus admired this deeply. Socrates was not a system-builder. He was a **presence** — one that could not be absorbed by the state.

But the moment passed. Plato systematized Socratic tension into metaphysical clarity. The world became divided into appearances and forms. Justice became geometry. Knowledge became hierarchy. Aristotle followed with even greater precision — virtue was mapped, logic was formalized, the search for purpose took on a taxonomic shape.

Camus respected their brilliance. But he had no need for their scaffolding.

He did not want a world that made sense through design. He wanted to live in a world that didn't — and still remain free.

He shared Socrates' refusal. But he did not follow the path the post-Socratics took — the path that turned that original refusal

Chapter 17: Western Philosophical Systems

into doctrine. His answer was to keep the question open, not to close it with a system.

Cynicism – The Theatrics of Refusal

Diogenes the Cynic lived in a barrel. He carried a lantern in daylight, searching for an honest man. He urinated in public. He insulted Alexander the Great. His life was a kind of performance — a living critique of corruption, wealth, and convention.

Some have drawn a line from Diogenes to Camus: both refused power, both rejected systems, both exposed hypocrisy.

But Camus was not Diogenes.

Where Diogenes performed contempt, Camus practiced restraint. Where Diogenes mocked the world, Camus mourned it. Camus did not seek to shock. He sought to endure. His rebellion was not theatrical. It was moral.

He may have admired the ferocity of Diogenes. But he never confused rage with clarity.

Stoicism – The Closest Parallel

Stoicism, rooted in ancient Greece and Rome, taught that virtue lay in accepting fate, living according to reason, and cultivating inward composure. It distrusted emotion and elevated serenity. Pain was to be endured. The world, however cruel, was still rational.

Camus admired Stoicism — but he did not join it.

He shared its rejection of complaint, its suspicion of self-pity, and its emphasis on dignity. His characters — Meursault, Jacques' mother, Dr. Rieux — often endure without spectacle. But Camus was not seeking serenity. He was seeking lucidity.

Where Stoicism trusted the order of nature, Camus saw indifference. Where Stoicism preached detachment, Camus remained rooted in care.

And going forward? Camus did not progress toward stillness so much as he moved toward warmth. *The First Man* is not a Stoic text — it is textured, embodied, unresolved. His posture remained internally coherent, but it no longer sought composure. It sought presence.

Skepticism – Doubt Without Paralysis

Ancient Skeptics suspended judgment. They held that certainty was impossible and peace lay in refusing to assert what could not be known.

Camus shared their suspicion of systems. But he was not passive.

He did not suspend judgment. He acted in its absence.

Skeptics waited for clarity. Camus moved forward without it. His was not the doubt that retreats. It was the doubt that **walks on**.

He never pretended to know what he could not. But he never used unknowing as an excuse to avoid responsibility — or to avoid acting when action meant refusal.

Why These Roots Matter

Camus carried these traditions with him — but loosely.

He was shaped by their questions, but not held by their answers.

In his final years, Camus was not drawing conclusions. He was shedding them. What began as rebellion became rhythm. What

Chapter 17: Western Philosophical Systems

began as critique became poise. His relationship to the philosophical tradition was not to conclude it — but to **decline its invitation**.

He walked with its echoes. And then, he moved beyond them.

Chapter 18: Eastern Thought Systems

Camus never studied the East in depth — but by the end of his life, he had begun to resemble it.

Camus encountered Eastern traditions — Taoism, Buddhism, Hindu texts — but never in a sustained or systematic way. His writings and Lottman's biography contain scattered references: Chuang Tzu, Buddha, Hindu books, even a plaster Khmer Buddha on his bedroom shelf.[29] These were glances, not studies. Yet in the final motion of his life, his temperament began to echo themes long held in the East. He no longer sought to clarify the world. He sought to dwell within it.

This chapter is not a claim of influence — it is an observation of **convergence**. Camus, by temperament and by trajectory, arrived at gestures long held in the East — gestures that are not conclusions, as they are in much of Western philosophy, but beginnings: presence, contradiction, the dignity of silence, the endurance of what is.

We explore not his knowledge of these systems, but how his lived stance came to **echo them**.

Taoism – Harmony Without Assertion

Taoism, particularly in the writings of Laozi and Zhuangzi, invites a life of balance, non-interference, and natural rhythm.

---

[29] Camus acquired the plaster Khmer Buddha in 1935, during his first marriage, when Jean de Maisonseul (his closest friend at the time) designed the couple's bedroom. The object's significance is uncertain; it may have been chosen for aesthetic rather than philosophical reasons.

It rejects the rigid structures of human ambition and urges a return to the effortless flow of the Tao — the Way.

Camus did not know the Tao. But in his final work, he moved like someone who had stopped resisting the current.

He never advocated passivity. He rejected nihilism. But like the Taoists, he came to understand that meaning is not imposed — it is encountered. Not extracted. Not defended. Simply walked with.

The *First Man* is not a treatise. It is a movement through memory, soil, light. There is no call to action. There is only return. Stillness. Exactness. A man who no longer needs to win in order to be free.

In that way, Camus was not becoming Eastern. He was becoming whole.

Zen Buddhism – The End of Explanation

Zen does not seek to define truth. It seeks to exhaust the need for definitions. Its method is not analysis but interruption — paradox, silence, sudden confrontation — breaking the pattern of grasping after answers.

Camus did not practice Zen. But by the end of his life, he no longer reached for explanation.

Philosophers of his era — Sartre, de Beauvoir, and before them Kierkegaard — had explored this condition of contradiction: the human hunger for clarity, meaning, and order confronted by the unresponsiveness of the universe. Camus named this tension *the absurd* in his early work and insisted it must be faced without illusion. In *The Myth of Sisyphus*, he writes: "There is no fate that cannot be surmounted by scorn."

Chapter 18: Eastern Thought Systems

The absurd had once required a response — defiance, revolt, clarity. But in his final posture, it became something else: a condition to be named, then moved through. Not ignored. Not solved. Simply acknowledged.

This was not resignation. It was lucid peace — what Zen might call the clarity of no-position.

Camus didn't sit on a cushion. But he stood in the world with that same stillness. He stopped trying to defy what could not be repaired or changed, and began to live with what could still be honored.

Vedanta – The Dissolution of Division

Vedantic thought, as expressed in the Upanishads, speaks of a self that is not separate from the world. Atman is Brahman. The individual, properly seen, is not cut off from reality, but rooted in its wholeness.

Camus did not believe in divine unity. He would have rejected the metaphysics. And yet — he did reject fragmentation. He resisted the broken logic of a world that divides man from meaning, self from setting, mind from body.

In *The First Man*, Camus begins to integrate. Memory, dirt, sun, and loss — all come together as part of a single life. There is no longer a separate self railing against absurdity. There is only a man remembering his mother's hands and the taste of salt air.

Camus does not merge with the cosmos. But he does cease to fight it.

Confucianism – Dignity in the Everyday

Confucian thought does not traffic in absolutes. It teaches ethics not through commandments, but through attentiveness to roles, rituals, and relationships. Harmony is not abstract. It is lived—in how one speaks, listens, and remembers.

Camus shared this modesty.

He believed that morality was not a declaration, but a discipline. Not a grand philosophy, but a posture held over time. In *The First Man*, the weight of love is found not in words, but in the quiet endurance of his mother. Her silence is not lack. It is substance.

Confucian wisdom lives in that silence.

Why These Echoes Matter

Schopenhauer was one of the first major Western philosophers to engage Eastern metaphysics – particularly with Hinduism and Buddhism, especially Vedanta. He read the Upanishads and praised the Buddha. Yet he often treated Eastern traditions as supporting artifacts for his already-formed pessimism. His interest, though sincere, was never embodied. He was, in many ways, a tourist — passing through traditions older than his own, gathering reflections that echoed the pessimism he already held.

Camus was not an Eastern thinker. But by the end of his life, he no longer needed to explain himself in Western terms. He was not synthesizing the traditions. He was letting them fall away.

What remained was a man — lucid, grounded, undeceived.

In the East, wisdom is often carried not in systems, but in gestures.
By the end, Camus was no longer building ideas. He was leaving gestures.

Chapter 18: Eastern Thought Systems

Not instructions.
Not answers.
Just a rhythm.

And in that rhythm, there is more kinship with Laozi, with a Zen monk, or with a silent Confucian elder than with any of the philosophers who shared his time.

Camus did not imitate the East. But he ended in a tone that parallels its settled confidence.

Chapter 19: An Invitation

Not an ending, but a way of continuing.

We have said the same thing many times.

That repetition was not accidental. It was a way of staying close. Camus does not yield to summary. He must be approached from different sides.

Each section, each pivot, each return has traced the edge of something—not to define it, but to dwell in its vicinity. This was never a project of explanation. It was an act of presence.

Camus did not offer conclusions. He offered gestures. Where the philosophical logician demanded, "There must be a system!" Camus turned to stepped into the open air and said,. "There must be a breeze". He stood a certain way, spoke with a certain clarity, and resisted certain illusions. And like all gestures, they ask not to be analyzed — but inhabited.

If there is an image to hold, perhaps it is this:

In the forest of philosophical thought, Camus seemed always to be standing at the edge of each clearing – at the treeline, where the light met the shade – and watched.
He understood that clarity lives at the edge — where one can see without being consumed.
The treeline offered a vantage, a place to attend to life without performing it.
He remained there, intact.

He had spent much of his life in tension with the absurd — naming it, refusing false consolations, insisting on lucidity. That tension shaped his most famous works: *The Myth of Sisyphus, The Stranger, The Plague, The Rebel.* But something changed. By the time of *The First Man*, he no longer needed to defend clarity. He had become it.

The absurd had not vanished. But it no longer required confrontation. It became part of the terrain, no longer an adversary. A presence, not a problem.

Schopenhauer had praised the Upanishads and admired the Buddha. But his relationship with Eastern thought remained aesthetic — curious, detached, speculative.

Camus made no sustained reference to Eastern traditions. But by the end of his life, he stood in a posture recognizable to them.

Still. Grounded. Undeceived.

Not explaining. Not defending. Simply being.

That is where this book finds its title. *Beyond the First Man* does not mean continuing the narrative. It means continuing the direction. Camus had already moved beyond his earlier defiance. He had turned toward something deeper — toward integration, rootedness, and presence.

The work was incomplete. But the trajectory was clear.

And now the page is handed to us.

This is not a conclusion. It is an invitation.

To stand where you are. To speak only what is yours to say. To live without excuse.

Camus asked for no disciples. He left no commandments. But he showed us what it looked like to remain at the treeline — clear-eyed, unshaken, and whole.

Chapter 19: An Invitation

The page turns. And you are still here.

That is enough.

www.ingramcontent.com/pod-product-compliance
Lightning Source LLC
Chambersburg PA
CBHW032041040426
42449CB00007B/974